BUILDING RAISED BEDS

Easy, Accessible Garden Space for Vegetables and Flowers

Fern Marshall Bradley

Storey Publishing

*The mission of Storey Publishing is to serve our customers by
publishing practical information that encourages
personal independence in harmony with the environment.*

Edited by Sarah Guare and Carleen Madigan
Series design by Alethea Morrison
Art direction by Jeff Stiefel
Text production by Theresa Wiscovitch
Indexed by Christine R. Lindemer, Boston Road Communications

Cover illustration by © Lisel Ashlock
Interior illustrations by © Elayne Sears

Storey books are available for special premium and promotional uses and for cus-
tomized editions. For further information, please call 1-800-793-9396.

Storey Publishing
210 MASS MoCA Way
North Adams, MA 01247
www.storey.com

Printed in the United States by McNaughton & Gunn, Inc.
10 9 8 7 6 5 4 3 2 1

LIBRARY OF CONGRESS CATALOGING-IN-PUBLICATION DATA

Names: Bradley, Fern Marshall, author.
Title: Building raised beds : easy, accessible garden space for vegetables
  and flowers / Fern Marshall Bradley.
Other titles: Easy, accessible garden space for vegetables and flowers
Description: North Adams, MA : Storey Publishing, [2015]
Identifiers: LCCN 2015035872| ISBN 9781612126166 (pbk. : alk. paper) | ISBN
  9781612126173 (ebook)
Subjects: LCSH: Beds (Gardens)—Design and construction. | Raised bed
  gardening.
Classification: LCC SB423.7 .B73 2015 | DDC 635.9/62—dc23 LC record available at
  http://lccn.loc.gov/2015035872

CONTENTS

THE BUILT-IN BENEFITS OF RAISED BEDS

Most of us have a favorite photo or painting hanging on the wall at home, mounted in a nice frame. There's something satisfying and pleasing about a framed picture. The frame sets off the image from its surroundings, announcing it as something special.

Creating raised beds for a garden works the same magic. Elevating a garden bed several inches above ground level calls attention to the plants growing there. Whether you frame the bed with wood or bricks, or simply cover up the exposed soil at the sides with grass clippings or wood shavings, the finished result looks great.

The lovely appearance of raised beds can motivate you to take good care of your garden all season long, but that's just one of the benefits of gardening in raised beds. Growing in raised beds offers important growing advantages to the plants and helpful logistic advantages for gardeners, too. Raised beds are:

- Sized right for success
- Perfectly designed for super soil
- Ready to plant right from the start
- Easy to expand

SIZED RIGHT FOR SUCCESS

WHAT'S THE RIGHT SIZE for a vegetable garden? In most cases, smaller than you might think. It's surprising how much food a garden as small as 100 square feet can produce.

Many new gardeners make the mistake of starting too large, because it's easy to map out a large ground-level garden plot and till it up. Creating such a garden plot happens fast, but the work needed to plant, tend, and harvest a big garden adds up over the season. If your garden is larger than you can manage, it's all too easy to fall behind your planting schedule. Weeds will sprout, and the task of fighting weeds will become a chore. Or you may have too much success, with such a large harvest that you don't have enough time to pick it all, let alone freeze or can the abundance.

Setting up a raised-bed garden takes more planning, time, and effort than starting a ground-level garden, and that's a positive! You'll be more likely to start out small, and starting out at the right scale has benefits that last all season long. You won't fall behind on planting, and you'll remain motivated to water and tend to your plants. You'll harvest crops at the perfect time, allowing you to enjoy maximum flavor and freshness. You'll have time to sow cover crops and make compost, which will improve the soil and lead to even better results as years go by.

PERFECTLY DESIGNED FOR SUPER SOIL

BECOMING A GOOD GARDENER is as much about learning how to nurture the soil as it is about learning how to tend crops. Loose, fertile, *living* soil is what vegetable and flowering plants need, and the process of building a raised bed is a wonderful opportunity to create just that kind of soil environment. You may be lucky enough to have high-quality soil, in which case you can work directly with your existing soil to shape raised beds. But if you have problem soil that is low in nutrients, drains poorly, or is full of rocks (there will be more on how to determine your soil type on page 9), you can garden in raised beds built on top of the native soil. Simply spread a base layer of newspaper or cardboard over the ground surface and build up, using enriched purchased topsoil or compost instead.

Raised-bed gardening protects soil quality over time because you can tend your garden without ever having to step on the soil in the beds. You'll sit, stand, or kneel in permanent pathways between the beds instead. This allows the soil in the beds to retain a loose, open structure with lots of pore space, which allows air and water to penetrate the soil easily. That provides ideal conditions for both the plant roots and the beneficial microorganisms that help supply the nutrients plants need for healthy growth.

READY TO PLANT RIGHT FROM THE START

THE TEMPERATURE OF GARDEN SOIL can vary from freezing in winter to as high as 100°F (38°C) on a hot summer day. Why does soil temperature matter? It matters because it affects both seed germination and root growth. The ideal soil temperature for germination of many vegetable crops is in the range of 50 to 70°F (10–20°C). Some types of seeds will germinate at lower temperatures, but they'll be more prone to rot or to develop slowly, which can affect yield down the line.

At the start of the gardening season in spring, soil is cold and usually wet. That's discouraging for gardeners eager to start the season! Sowing seeds may be an exercise in futility, and digging in soil when it's wet can lead to problems, too — it can ruin soil structure, which is bad both for soil organisms and for plant roots.

The good news: the soil in raised beds tends to be drier and warmer than the soil in ground-level beds. For one thing, water drains easily in the loose, open soil of a raised bed, and drier soil heats up more quickly than wet soil does. And because the bed is raised, spring sunshine has more of a warming effect on it. The bed can absorb heat not only through the top surface but also through the sides. (You can enhance the warming effect by framing a raised bed with stones, which will absorb heat during the day and release it to the soil in the bed at night.) If you garden in the north, you may find a dramatic difference between the soil temperature in your raised beds and the soil temperature in the surrounding soil — 10°F (5.5°C) or more. Add to that the fact that soil in a raised bed is loose and open (because it's not compacted by foot traffic), and even in early spring it's possible to gently open shallow furrows for seeds and dig planting holes for seedlings without damaging soil structure. And the warmer soil will mean you can keep on gardening later in the fall, too.

You can build a raised bed at any time of year when the soil isn't frozen. Summer and fall are ideal times, because you'll be less busy with planting than you are in spring, and you can choose a day when conditions are pleasant for working outdoors. After you build the new bed, you can plant it right

Attention Gardeners in Arid Climates

A word of caution for gardeners in arid climates: raised beds are prone to drying out more quickly than in-ground gardens. That's not a benefit when water is scarce. Keep that in mind when you design your garden. You may do better to take the opposite approach and design a sunken-bed garden rather than a raised-bed one.

away, or you can cover the soil surface with a protective layer of leaves or straw, and it will be ready for you whenever you're ready to plant.

EASY TO EXPAND

As you gain gardening experience, you may decide you need more growing space, especially if you want to start growing more space-hogging crops such as tomatoes or butternut squash, or start a small bed of flowering ornamentals. The beauty of a raised-bed garden is that you can add as many beds as your property allows. You can build an additional bed alongside your existing beds or anyplace in your yard where conditions are favorable for growing. Because raised beds are naturally appealing to the eye, they're a good choice for a garden even in the front yard.

As you add beds, you may want to experiment with different sizes and shapes. You could plant a shallow raised bed along a fence and train crops up onto the fence. You might want to build a circular or oval bed, or try a double-decker bed. The possibilities with raised beds are wide open!

CHAPTER ONE

GETTING STARTED

The best time to set up a raised-bed garden is whenever you have the time to make a garden plan and put it in action (although you can't build a raised bed when the soil is frozen). The first step is to find the right site. Next, evaluate the soil there and decide whether to loosen it for planting or leave it intact and build a bed from the ground level up. Plan the layout of the bed or beds and what kind of frame you'll use, if any.

The final step is deciding whether your garden will be a solo do-it-yourself project, whether you'll enlist the help of family or friends, or whether you'll hire some help. There's some heavy lifting involved in the beginning phase of most raised-bed projects. But once your beds are built, tending them is generally light work for all the years that follow.

INVESTIGATING SUNLIGHT AND SOIL

IF YOU'RE PLANNING TO CONVERT an existing vegetable garden to raised beds, then your choice of site is already made. But if you're starting from scratch, look for the sunniest spot you can find, because most vegetable crops grow best in bright sunshine. Lettuce and a few other crops can tolerate light shade, but the best site is one that receives at least 6 hours of direct sun per day, especially during the middle of the day.

Siting for Sun

Choose a sunny day to investigate your site. In the morning, use bricks or rocks to mark the corners of an imagined garden site; then return throughout the day to observe the sun and shade patterns. Make adjustments in the position of the bed if needed. Consider how the patterns will change over the course of the gardening season, too. In summer, the sun is high in the sky, so shadows are minimal. The sun is lower (closer to south) during spring and fall, so trees and buildings cast longer shadows that might extend across your garden site.

If your surroundings include lots of trees or buildings that block sun, your yard may offer only isolated pools of sunlight. If that's the case, you can set up a single raised bed in each pool. There's no rule that beds have to be grouped together. A group of beds is more convenient to tend, but sun trumps all when it comes to growing veggies and most flowering annuals — so set up beds wherever the sunlight is available. If some parts of your yard are always in shade, you can still grow many beautiful perennials there, including hostas, violas, pulmonarias, and astilbes. These will thrive in a shady raised bed.

What if you find that the sunniest site available is a driveway or patio? If you don't mind giving up a portion of the paved area, you can work with the site by setting up a sturdy frame and filling it with a growing mix such as compost mixed with peat and sand. Be aware that the surface underneath may degrade over time. If you decide to remove the bed in the future, you may find the paved surface is pitted or stained.

Checking the Soil

Soil seems solid; after all, when you walk across a lawn or along a woodland path, you're walking on soil, and it feels firm under your feet (unless it's been raining hard and the soil has turned to mud). When you take a closer look at soil, though, you'll find that it's not solid like wood or stone. Rather, soil is made up of myriad tiny particles; bits of rock worn down through centuries become soil.

TYPES OF SOIL

Technically speaking, there are three types of particles in soil, and they're defined by their size. The largest group of particles is called sand, the middle group is called silt, and the smallest group is called clay. The relative proportions of these particles affect the qualities of soil: how fast it dries out, how easy it is to dig, and how well it holds nutrients that plants need for growth. For example, sandy soil dries out faster than clay soil. A soil that has a fairly even balance of all three types of particles is called loamy soil. Loamy soil can be ideal for gardening, but it's possible to grow great plants in clay and sandy soil, too. Adding organic matter will help a lot to improve the water-holding capacity of sandy soil and to loosen up clay soil.

Once you've picked your site, dig a little hole to check out the soil. Scoop some soil into your hand and rub it between your fingers. A handful of soil can feel sandy, or it may feel like a loose powder (silt), or it may feel sticky (clay).

ORGANIC MATTER AND BENEFICIAL ORGANISMS

More important than these mineral particles is the living component of soil. As you dig in the soil, you'll see some living things such as plant roots, earthworms, beetles, and centipedes. In addition, you'll see formerly living material — dead leaves, bits of plant stem, and old roots — which gardeners call organic matter.

There's also a universe of living organisms in the soil that you can't see: bacteria, fungi, nematodes, and more. These living creatures are the most critical aspect of soil for gardeners. They digest nutrients in organic matter and transform them into substances that plant roots can absorb; in other words, they turn organic matter into plant food. Your work as a gardener is to provide a hospitable haven for these beneficial microbes.

If you don't see any signs of life in your soil, that's a cause for concern, but it's a problem you can fix by adding organic matter in the form of compost and by mulching (covering) the soil surface with organic materials such as shredded leaves. There's more information about improving the organic matter content of soil later in this book (see page 39).

Soil Science

There's an incredible amount of life humming away in the soil, at a scale that can't be seen by human eyes. The interactions in the soil are fascinating to learn about. And the more you discover about soil biology, the better gardener you'll become. Here are some amazing details:

- Many types of vegetables (and other plants) are dependent on specialized soil fungi called *mycorrhizae* for optimal growth. These fungi send out a network of weblike threads into the soil to mine nutrients from a much larger area than a plant's roots can reach on their own. These fungi may or may not be naturally present in your soil, but you can buy *inoculants* that contain these fungi and mix them into the soil at planting time (see Resources, page 87, for sources of inoculants).

- Some types of plant diseases are caused by bacteria and fungi that live in the soil and invade plant roots. But there are also beneficial bacteria and fungi that work to keep out these invaders by forming a natural barrier around the root zone or by feeding on the harmful species.

- Plants seem to understand how vital beneficial soil bacteria and fungi are. Plants make sugars in their leaves (via photosynthesis), and they send a portion of those sugars down through stems into their roots and out into the soil to create an energy-rich zone where microbes can feed. Microbes use the energy they gain to break down organic matter into substances rich in nitrogen, potassium, phosphorus, and other elements that plants need to build new plant cells.

To discover more fascinating facts about what's happening in the soil, see Resources, page 87.

DRAINAGE

Like most living things, plant roots and soil-dwelling organisms need air (specifically oxygen) in order to live and grow. That's why soil drainage is so important. Some soils, especially those with lots of clay, don't drain well: water tends to stay trapped in the surface soil, filling all the pore spaces, which can suffocate plant roots.

To test drainage, dig a hole at your site about 1 foot deep and 1 foot wide. Use your garden hose to fill the hole with water. Let that water drain away completely; then turn on the hose and fill the hole again. Note the time or set a timer; then check the hole now and again until all the water has drained away (it will likely take hours). If the hole isn't empty within 8 hours, the soil drains poorly. Building a raised bed and filling it with purchased topsoil or compost is a great solution to poorly drained soil. The bed should be at least 6 inches deep to allow space for roots to grow and thrive above the heavy natural soil underneath the bed.

No soil is perfect, and while digging a hole for a drainage test, you may discover other problems, such as an abundance of rocks, very sandy soil, or a wild proliferation of persistent weed roots. The good news is that many soil problems can be lessened simply by adding organic matter. And if your site has soil with a difficult problem, you can choose simply to cover over the existing soil with cardboard or newspapers to block weed growth and build your raised garden from the ground level up.

DIG DOWN OR BUILD UP?

ONE APPROACH TO STARTING raised beds involves loosening the soil and heaping it up into low mounds. The other basic bed-building method employs a solid frame constructed at ground level and filled with materials gathered off-site. Both approaches require some physical labor, and both have pros and cons. You'll make the decision whether to dig down or build up based on the soil characteristics of your site, the type of plants already growing there, and your budget.

If your soil doesn't have any major problems, it's a good idea to dig down; that way, you'll avoid the cost of buying topsoil or soil mix to fill the beds. But if your soil has a major problem, such as poor drainage or contamination by lead or other pollutants, it's best to build frames and fill them with topsoil or compost. Building beds at least 1 foot tall offers the advantage of allowing you to tend the beds without stooping over.

DIMENSIONS AND LAYOUT

BEFORE YOU START DIGGING or building frames, draw a layout plan for your garden. How many beds will there be, and what dimensions?

Bed Width

Start by deciding on bed width. Get down on your knees and pretend you're reaching out with one arm to plant seeds or pick beans from a garden bed. How far can you reach without straining? For most people, the comfortable distance is 18 to 24 inches. Measure your own comfortable reach and multiply that distance by 2 — that's the maximum bed width for your garden. (If you're designing a bed along alongside a fence or wall, don't multiply by 2, because your access to the bed will be limited to just one side.) A bed that exceeds your reach will lead to the temptation to step onto the bed while you work, and that negates one of the primary goals of raised-bed gardening: maintaining loose, airy soil.

Bed Length

Bed length is a more personal choice than bed width. It may depend on the overall shape of your garden site. For a square site, a grid of four beds may work well. For a long and narrow site, consider lining up three beds in a single row. Take care not to make beds *too* long, or you'll end up frustrated by the repetitious walk around the end of the bed to get to the other side (more temptation to step onto the bed to shortcut across). If you're a beginning gardener, it's a good idea to start out with beds of a standard size, such as 4 feet × 8 feet.

Orientation to the Sun

In midsummer, when the sun is high overhead, there's very little shade in a vegetable garden. But in spring and late summer, the sun doesn't travel as high in the sky and tall garden crops can cast shade on the plants on their north side. Consider this when you're deciding how to orient your beds. Should the long dimension run north to south, or east to west? Both

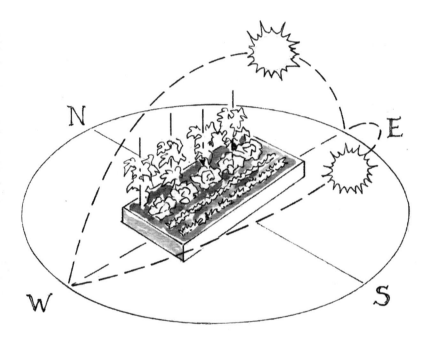

BEDS SET UP WITH a north-south orientation are fine for crops of equal height, but for a combination of tall and short crops, choose an east-west orientation. To prevent one crop from shading another, plant tall crops along the north edge of the bed, with shorter crops in the center and along the south edge of the bed.

north-south beds and east-west beds can work well, as long as you're aware of which direction is north and plant accordingly to avoid shading crops, as shown on page 15. Occasionally, creating shade in a vegetable garden has advantages. For example, if tall tomato plants create a lightly shaded spot, that can be a perfect place to plant a summer crop of lettuce, which benefits from some shade during peak summer heat.

Pathways

As you map your layout, be generous with path width. Pathways between raised beds serve more than one purpose. They're your workstation — the place where you will stand, sit, or kneel while you tend your garden. They're the spot where you'll put your bucket of work tools and supplies, and your harvest basket of produce. And they'll be the highway and the parking spot for a wheelbarrow full of compost or transplants. Be sure your garden pathways are wide enough to accommodate all that activity. In most cases, 2 feet is the minimum comfortable width for pathways between raised beds.

three beds in a row

four-square grid

offset

THREE BEDS IN A ROW is a fine layout for a raised-bed garden. A four-square grid of beds works well around a central compost pile or tub garden of herbs and flowers. You can offset beds for an artful effect or to match the footprint of a limited area of full sun.

CHAPTER TWO

BUILDING YOUR BEDS

With your garden plan prepared, it's time for the work-intensive stage of gardening in raised beds: building the beds themselves. If you're creating beds with native soil, that means digging or tilling. If you're building a framed bed, you'll need to buy materials, gather tools, and assemble the frames. There are some shortcuts you can take to save time and labor, but it's a good idea to set aside a full day or a weekend for a bed-building project.

DIGGING DOWN

BUILDING RAISED BEDS with native soil is less costly than filling frames with purchased soil materials, but there's no doubt it requires more physical labor. It's important to clear the soil surface of weedy growth before you begin digging.

Removing Surface Growth

Before you dig, you may need to remove the surface vegetation, especially if the site is covered with lawn grass or weeds. Mark the outside perimeter of the overall garden, and then use a sharp spade to cut through the surface vegetation vertically to isolate a strip. When you've cut a strip the width of the garden, slide the blade of the spade horizontally underneath the sod at one end of the strip and slice through the roots. As you work, you can roll up the strip of sod or simply cut and lift squares, as shown on page 20.

Put the removed sod into a wheelbarrow and take it to your composting area; it will eventually break down into compost. (For more about making compost, see page 39.)

Assessing Soil Moisture

After you've removed surface vegetation and before you turn the soil, check soil moisture. If the soil is too dry or too wet, turning it will cause serious damage to the soil's natural structure — damage that is difficult to repair. If the soil is too dry, water it or wait for rain. If it's too wet, check it daily until it's dried out a bit. Test soil moisture by squeezing a handful of soil in your fist. If the soil sticks together in a muddy ball, it's too wet. If it feels dusty dry, it's too dry. If it forms a ball that crumbles apart into smaller pieces, it's just right.

REMOVE SOD one square at a time, or roll up a strip. The strip may be heavy to move!

Turning the Soil

You can dig the bed by hand or turn the soil with a rotary tiller. There's no denying that hand-digging a garden bed is heavy labor, but you can make it less arduous by breaking up the job over time. If, for example, a garden is 30 square feet, and you allow five days, then you have to dig only 6 square feet per day — that's less than the surface area of a standard card table.

To dig an entire garden in a day, though, using a tiller may be the only realistic choice. If you don't own a tiller, it's easy to find one to rent. Ask at a local garden center or hardware store. You can also "rent" labor, perhaps from your kids or the neighbor's teenage children, to dig a bed by hand, or you can probably find someone locally who owns a tiller and will do custom tilling for hire. Or throw a gardening potluck: you provide all the food, and your guests bring along their own shovel, digging fork, or rake. Take turns digging and eating!

However you decide to approach the task of turning the soil, be moderate. Turning the soil is a necessary step for creating a raised bed, but it's not a soil-friendly process. Turning the soil disrupts the natural structure of the soil, ruining it (in the short term) as a habitat for the organisms, both macro and micro, that call the soil home. The more you pulverize the soil, the more soil life is destroyed. But once you've shaped the raised beds, there are steps you can take to encourage microbes and other beneficial organisms to recolonize the soil. And keep in mind that the digging/tilling process is a one-time evil. From here on, you should never again have to dramatically disrupt the soil in your raised beds.

Smothering Sod

It's possible to get rid of sod or weed cover without physically cutting and removing it, but it takes time. If you can afford to wait two months before making your raised beds, you can smother the plant growth on your garden site by covering it with a heavy, dark, moisture-proof cover.

First, "scalp" the surface: use a mower or string trimmer to cut the grass or weeds as short as possible. Then cover the area with cardboard or newspapers, and top that with a sheet of heavy black plastic or a heavy-duty tarp. Weigh down the plastic or tarp securely with rocks, bricks, or scrap lumber.

Let the site sit undisturbed for at least a month, then remove the weights from one corner of the plot and lift the coverings. Is there any green plant growth underneath? If so, let the site rest 2 weeks longer and check again. Once all the surface vegetation is dead, you can open up the site and rake it clear (compost the material you rake off). Check soil moisture! If the site is too dry to turn (see page 19), water it well and then wait a couple of days for it to reach the right moisture level before you dig or till.

This type of treatment is very effective for killing tough weeds, but it's also hard on the beneficial organisms that live in soil. To help the soil rebound, be sure to add a biological activator or some rich mature compost to the bed before you plant.

Shaping the Beds

After you've worked the soil by tilling or digging, the next step is to shape the beds. First, gather the tools and equipment you'll need: your garden plan, a tape measure, stakes and string, a hammer, a garden rake, a shovel, a digging fork, and soil amendments. It's good to have a helper to assist with marking out the beds.

1. Following your garden plan, use your tape measure to determine the location of the four corners of each bed and hammer in a stake at each corner. Run string between the stakes.

2. Shape the beds by using your garden rake to pull soil out of the pathway areas onto the beds. You can rake the soil right up and over the strings. Move about a 2-inch depth of soil out of each pathway onto the beds. For unframed beds, it's best to limit bed height to about 4 inches; otherwise, the bed edges will slump and erode over time.

3. With your shovel, spread soil amendments such as com-
    post, lime, and kelp meal over the surface of the beds.
    (See page 39 for information on which amendments
    to use and in what quantities.) Caution: Many types
    of soil amendments are dusty. To protect your sinuses
    and lungs, wear a dust mask while working with soil
    amendments.

4. Use your digging fork to lightly mix the amendments
    into the top few inches of soil.

5. Back to the rake. Flip it over so the tines face up, and
    pull and push the rake over the surface of the bed to
    smooth and level the soil.

THESE SIMPLE RAISED BEDS took some time and energy to create, but
they will never need digging again. Each season, simply "fluff" the soil
lightly and plant!

BUILDING UP

BUILDING A RAISED BED from ground level up can be a relatively simple or fairly complex project, depending on the size and height of the bed. The minimum height for a framed bed is about 6 inches, because vegetable crops need to extend their roots about that deep in order to grow well and produce a good yield. Deeper is even better. Providing only 6 inches of soil compared to 12 inches is like giving your plants a mediocre diet of prepared foods rather than fresh home-cooked meals: it's harder to make optimum growth when the food supply isn't as plentiful or nutritious. That said, a 6-inch-deep raised bed filled with good-quality compost will give satisfactory results for most vegetable crops.

The frame should be made from a solid material such as wood, cinder blocks, or pavers. You can build your own frame from scratch or buy a prefabricated kit.

The best part about building up a raised bed is that there's no digging involved! That doesn't mean no heavy lifting, though, because you will have to fill the frame with soil or compost. As with the digging-down method, it's your choice whether to undertake the hauling and hefting yourself or hire help.

Choosing Frame Materials

Use your ingenuity in choosing materials to frame raised beds. Wood is a common choice because it's so easily available, but you can also use stones, cinder blocks, or straw bales.

WOOD

Plain old wooden boards work fine for framing raised beds. You can buy 2 × 6 pine boards from any home center or lumber yard, or seek out more rot-resistant wood such as cedar, white oak, black locust, or redwood. Keep in mind that the rot-resistant woods will be more expensive than pine.

Scrounged scrap lumber can serve the purpose, but only if you are certain that it is not treated wood. Treated wood is not suitable for raised-bed frames because the chemicals used to impregnate the wood can leach out into the soil. Other types of found wood may work, too, such as old dresser drawers, but be sure they are solid wood, not plywood or particle board (these are also impregnated with chemicals), and avoid painted wood.

Is rot-resistant wood worth the extra cost? That depends in part on your climate. Wood breaks down more quickly when it's wet than when it's dry, so rot-resistant wood is more important in regions that receive lots of rain. Composite (plastic) lumber is another long-lasting choice, but it's not as sturdy as real wood and may need more bracing to prevent the frame from being pushed out of shape by the weight of the soil inside it.

LOGS

Rough-cut logs can serve as a very attractive informal frame for raised beds. If you have a source for rough-cut logs, keep the bed size fairly small, 4 feet × 6 feet, for example, because longer logs will be very heavy to move. The logs will slowly decay, but they should last several years. A smooth log can be a nice place for you to sit while tending your garden.

STONE AND BLOCKS

A dry-laid stone wall can serve as the frame for a raised bed. If you plan to build a wall more than 1 foot tall, though, it will require mortar, or the weight of the soil could push the wall apart.

A stone frame around a low bed can be informal, too. In this case, you'd lay out smooth rocks roughly at the perimeter of the bed, fill up the bed, then push the rocks more firmly into place. The shape of the bed will shift and change a bit over time, but that's not a problem with a free-form bed — perhaps a roughly circular or oval bed. You may want to make a free-form bed wider than your reach. If you do this, you will have to step into the bed to reach some of the plants, so use large flat stones to make a pathway across the bed.

Cinder blocks are an inexpensive and nearly indestructible framing material, but their appearance is utilitarian and their surfaces can be rough on your hands as you tend the garden. Plus a single block weighs more than 40 pounds, so a cinder block bed is a building project that demands a lot of strength (or some good hired help).

Bricks or pavers can be a good choice. If you can find a source of used material, it will be low-cost or even free. If you choose bricks or pavers, you'll need to dig out a base layer and line it with crushed gravel to create a sturdy, level base that won't shift out of position. And for beds taller than 6 inches, you'll need to use mortar to hold a brick wall together.

CHOOSE A FRAME MATERIAL that suits your taste: clean-cut boards (top), rustic logs (middle), or durable cinder blocks (bottom) can all serve well to enclose raised beds.

KITS

Raised-bed kits range from small, simple plastic frames that can be snapped together without using tools to multidimensional cedar frames with built-in fencing to keep out animal pests. Pricing reflects the range of sizes, materials, and craftsmanship. You can buy a kit for a 4-foot × 8-foot frame for under $100 or invest up to $2,000 in a megakit. The cost for cedar frame kits ranges from $100 to $400, depending on bed height and length and the width of the framing lumber itself. You can shop for kits online or at garden centers and home centers.

It's worthwhile to investigate kits. You may decide that a kit is just the right time- and labor-saving approach for you, or you may be inspired by the simplicity of a kit design and decide you could easily build a bed just like it yourself!

STRAW BALES

A construction-free method for framing a bed is to use straw bales, which you can buy from a local farm or garden center. Simply set the bales in place at your garden site to make a rectangular frame, and then fill the opening with soil and organic materials. The bales make a comfortable spot to sit while you tend your beds (you may want to place a cushion to sit on, though, in case the straw is wet or stretchy). The bales will probably last two years, or longer in dry climates. As the bales decay, put a new set of bales around the bed and push them into place. The old straw is all organic matter that will help the soil life in the bed thrive.

Setting Up a Framed Bed

Once you've decided on your frame materials and design and are ready to set up your garden, mark the outlines of your beds with stakes and string and cut back the vegetation in the bed areas as close to ground level as possible. Don't cut the pathway areas, though, if you plan to leave them as sod paths. If you plan to cover your paths with wood chips or some other material, do cut the vegetation short.

Next, assemble your frame, which may take you one hour or several, depending on whether you're using a kit, a simple straw bale design, or wooden frames built from scratch. (See How to Build a Wood-Framed Raised Bed, page 33.) Whatever type of frame you're creating, it's a good idea to check the level of the assembled frame. Your frame doesn't need to be perfectly level, but if it's too far out of balance, it won't hold up as well as a level frame in the long run. You can scrape away soil if one corner of the frame is high, or tuck some crushed gravel under a low spot.

If your frame is only 6 inches tall, cover the ground surface inside the frame with cardboard (remove packaging tape from the cardboard first) or newspaper. Layer the newspaper several sheets thick. This will prevent grass and weeds from growing up through the soil in the frame. (Soil deeper than 6 inches should suppress nearly all plant growth.)

Filling a Framed Bed

What's the best filling for a framed raised bed? There are plenty of recipes to try.

COMPOST

One very good choice for filling is compost. It's rich in nutrients, usually has a balanced pH, and is appealing to soil-dwelling organisms. The trick is to find a reliable source of high-quality compost. If you're lucky enough to find a local supplier, put in your order as early as possible because they often sell out, especially during peak demand times such as late spring.

If you want to extend the compost, you can mix roughly equal quantities of compost, peat moss, and vermiculite. This is a classic recipe for filling raised beds, but keep in mind that many gardeners avoid peat moss because it's not a local, sustainably produced material. Also, this mix is not as nutrient-rich as compost alone, and you'll probably need to apply fertilizers during the growing season to keep plants thriving in a mix like this.

Beds filled with straight compost may noticeably shrink over time. Some of this is due to settling, but more of it is due to the soil life "digesting" the organic matter and using it to feed the plants. This is a good thing! But you will need a steady supply of compost to replenish the bed every year.

TOPSOIL

If you have a source of native soil that's suitable for gardening (perhaps you have good soil in parts of your yard that are too shady for gardening), you can dig it up and transport it by wheelbarrow to fill your beds. Or you can purchase topsoil in bulk from a landscaping supplier or sometimes a garden center. You can make a blend of 3 parts soil, 3 parts coarse sand, and

4 parts composted shredded leaves. Don't worry if you don't have these precise materials in these particular ratios. There's no single "right formula" for a raised-bed mix.

Beds filled with topsoil and amended with compost won't shrink as quickly as those filled with straight compost, but they will need a compost infusion each year to maintain fertility.

ARRANGING DELIVERY

Bagged compost or topsoil is available at most garden centers and home centers, but it may be cheaper or more convenient to arrange for a bulk delivery. Check for local suppliers and make sure you see a sample of the product before you place your order. Mature compost should be uniform rich brown to black, with no large chunks of undecomposed material. Be wary of topsoil that is too stony, or that contains visible pieces of perennial roots. Deliveries are usually quantified in cubic yards. One cubic yard is equal to 27 cubic feet. A 4-foot × 8-foot bed that is 10 inches deep would hold about 27 cubic feet, and a 4-foot × 12-foot bed would hold about 40 cubic feet.

Plan ahead for a bulk delivery. If the driver cannot maneuver the large, heavy dump truck right to your beds, scout out a level spot that the truck can reach, preferably at the same level or uphill from your beds, and as close to them as feasible. If you can't move the material immediately after the delivery, cover it with a tarp to prevent the soil or compost from becoming waterlogged by rain, which would make it much heavier and harder to work with.

It may be easiest to blend materials together right in the bed. Use your wheelbarrow (or a 5-gallon bucket or 10-gallon trash can) as your "measuring cup." Dump the ingredients into the bed, and then use a garden fork or small handheld tiller to mix them together.

HOW TO BUILD A WOOD-FRAMED RAISED BED

Designs abound for wood-framed raised beds, and frames made from 2 × 6, 2 × 8, or 2 × 12 boards or 4 × 4 timbers are very popular. The basic setup for a frame is the same for all of these materials, although the method for fastening the pieces together is different. Galvanized wood screws or nails are strong enough to hold together a frame made of 2 × 6s or 2 × 12s, but 6-inch-long galvanized spikes or timber screws are needed to connect 4 × 4s. The following materials and instructions are for a bed that is approximately 4 feet wide and 6 feet long with sides made from 2 × 6s. The sequence for assembling a frame of a different size made with different framing materials would be similar.

MATERIALS

- 2 × 6 lumber (two 12-foot lengths)
- 2 × 2 lumber or lumber scraps
- 3-inch galvanized wood screws or nails

TOOLS

- Tape measure
- Handsaw or circular saw
- Power drill (if using screws)
- Screwdriver or hammer
- Spirit level (optional)

(continued on next page)

1. Gather your materials and prepare the site by stripping off existing vegetation as described on page 20.

2. You'll need two 6-foot lengths for the long sides and two 3.75-foot (45-inch) lengths for the short sides. Measure the lengths with the tape measure, and use the saw to cut the boards.

3. Set the boards into position. If you're using screws, first use the power drill to make pilot holes in the wood. Then screw or hammer two pieces together at the corner. Or, you can cut lengths of 2 × 2 or scrap

   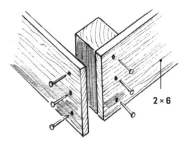

   lumber to serve as corner braces and drive nails or screws through the frame pieces directly into a brace.

4. Fasten together the other two frame boards at the opposite corner. Next, check to see if the frame is squarely aligned. One way to do this is to measure the distance diagonally across the frame, and then measure across the other diagonal. If the two distances are equal, then the corners are square. When you're sure the frame is squared up, add fasteners at the two remaining corner joints as well.

5. Use a spirit level to check that the frame is level, or simply get down on the ground and eyeball it for levelness. If there are high or low spots, add more soil or dig out soil as needed until the frame is level all around.

6. For beds that are longer than 6 feet, add a center brace to reinforce the frame and prevent the weight of the soil from distorting the shape of the frame over time. Or you can drive sturdy metal garden stakes into the soil along the outside face of the long sides of the frame and use screws to fasten the stakes to the framing.

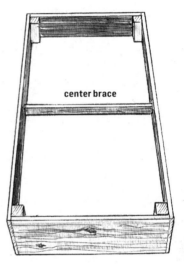

center brace

For taller frames that use a second set of boards or timbers, stagger the end joints. This makes for sturdier joints that are less likely to shift out of place over time. Fasten the two tiers together by driving spikes or screws down through the second course into the timbers below (you may need to drill pilot holes first).

HOW TO BUILD A FRAME ON A SLOPE

On a gently sloping site, a three-sided frame may fit better than a four-sided frame. In this case, you'll be working with the existing soil, and you'll first loosen the soil and roughly shape the beds and paths. Here's how to set up a three-sided frame to support the beds and prevent them from slumping down the slope. *Note:* Steeper slopes require more sophisticated designs and support to prevent the beds from collapsing.

These instructions are for 8-foot-long frames, but the instructions would be similar for frames of other lengths.

MATERIALS

- 2 × 12 lumber
- ½-inch rebar
- Coarse gravel
- 3-inch galvanized wood screws

TOOLS

- Tape measure
- Handsaw or circular saw
- Hacksaw
- Hammer or 1-pound sledge
- Power drill
- Hoe or rake

1. For the front face of the bed, use the tape measure to measure 8-foot lengths from the 2 × 12 lumber, and use the handsaw to cut the lengths. Use the hacksaw to cut the rebar into pieces approximately 1.5 feet (18 inches) long.

2. Put the face board in position (it's easier if you have a helper while doing this). Use the hammer to pound in the lengths of rebar about every 4 feet along the face board; the rebar will support the board and prevent the weight of soil from pushing the board off vertical. The rebar should extend at least 12 inches into the ground, and it should not extend above the top edge of the face board (for safety's sake).

3. Cut triangular side pieces (not more than 4 feet long), matching the angle of the cut to the approximate pitch of the slope.

4. Wedge the side boards into place, and (first using the power drill to make pilot holes) use the galvanized wood screws to attach the face board to the side pieces.

5. Use the hoe to pull soil up the slope, opening a small gap between the soil and the face board. Backfill that gap with gravel to lessen the effects of frost-heaving. (Frost

(continued on next page)

heaving is movement of the soil as it freezes and thaws in winter and early spring.)

IN A GARDEN ON A GENTLE SLOPE, frame the downhill face and sides of each bed. Support the downhill face with rebar to prevent it from tilting.

SOIL AMENDMENTS

SOIL AMENDMENTS are food for the soil: materials that boost soil organic matter and thus encourage healthy populations of soil microorganisms. It's important to add soil amendments when you first shape your beds because they will help initiate the healing process your soil needs after the disturbance from digging or tilling.

Compost

Compost, a diverse mix of decomposed organic materials, is the best soil amendment around. You may have a home-garden compost pile, but even if you don't, you can easily find local sources of compost. Ask your gardening friends and check Craigslist. All garden centers and home centers sell bagged compost, and you may discover a local farm or business that makes compost and offers bulk delivery.

Many municipalities offer compost to residents for free. Such compost is usually made from leaves, grass clippings, and other materials collected from around town and composted in bulk at the town's recycling site. This compost can be excellent in quality, or not so good. It can even be hazardous to your plants, because it may contain the residues of herbicides that have long-lasting effects. Such herbicides can cause stunting or deformed growth.

If you suspect that the compost you're using could be contaminated, test it before adding it to your raised beds. Set up an experiment with four small pots. Put potting soil in a couple of pots, and potting soil mixed with the compost in the other two. Sow three seeds of peas or beans in each pot and water them well. Put the pots in a warm, well-lit spot. Keep them watered as they germinate. Compare the appearance of the seedlings as they grow. If the leaves show distortions such as cupping (turning up of the leaf margins), wrinkling, or thickening, that's a sign of herbicide damage.

Lime and Sulfur

Soil pH is a measure of the level of acidity or alkalinity in the soil environment. It's expressed as a number, such as 7.0, which is the pH of a neutral soil. A pH lower than 7.0 tends toward acid, and a pH value higher than 7.0 tends toward alkaline. Most vegetable crops grow best in a pH range of 6.0 to 7.0. But in some regions of the country, soils are naturally acid, and in other areas they are naturally alkaline. If your soil falls outside the range of 6.0 to 7.0, you can change its pH by adding lime (to raise the pH) or sulfur (to lower the pH). However, the change doesn't happen instantly. It will take about 2 months after lime or sulfur is added for the chemical reactions in the soil to run their course and make the shift happen.

You can check soil pH using a simple test kit available at garden centers, or you can take a soil sample and have the pH tested. Ask at your local garden center or Cooperative Extension Service office about how to prepare a soil sample and have it tested.

The amount of lime or sulfur to add to change your soil's pH depends on the type of soil, but as a rough rule of thumb, 5 pounds of dolomitic lime per 100 square feet of garden bed mixed into the top 2 inches of soil will raise the pH by 1 point (for example, from 5.5 to 6.5). With iron sulfate, the rate is 1.5 pounds per 100 square feet to lower pH by 1 point.

Other Amendments

Choices of soil amendments are plentiful, and specific amendments help supply different nutrients that plants need, including nitrogen, phosphorus, potassium, magnesium, and calcium. For example, blood meal and fish meal are nitrogen sources. Bone meal and rock phosphate supply phosphorus. There's a lot to learn about soil amendments, and it is possible to overapply them. It's best not to add them unless you study up first, test your soil to see what nutrients are deficient, or get advice from a trusted source. For more information about soil amendments, see Resources, page 87. Don't worry, though. It's not essential to apply specific soil amendments. Generally, if you add compost each year, your soil will gradually improve over time. And you can monitor plant growth and use organic fertilizer during the growing season if your plants look peaked.

PATHWAYS

WITH YOUR BEDS IN PLACE, you'll be eager to start planting! Take time first, though, to finish preparing the pathways between the beds. When you start beds in a lawn area, it's a simple choice to leave your pathways as is. Grass pathways are comfortable to walk and kneel on, and they look attractive as long as you're willing to keep them trimmed. You may want to invest in a quality pair of grass shears for trimming the grass along the beds, in the spots you can't reach with your mower. And if your beds aren't framed, it's wise to edge the beds with a spade or half-moon edger twice a season to prevent grass from invading the beds.

Your other choice is to cover the pathways. You can use some type of mulch (such as bark chips, wood chips, or straw), or you can use gravel or pavers. Each type of covering has pros and cons. Bark/wood chips and straw are softer for kneeling than gravel or pavers, but they need to be renewed at least once per growing season. Gravel or pavers give the garden a more finished and elegant appearance, and weeds and grass will be less likely to push through them. However, installing gravel or paved paths is more work than spreading bark/wood chips or straw. Choose the material based on price, style preference, and comfort.

STEP AND PRESS DOWN firmly with your foot on a half-moon edger to cut cleanly through soil and roots at the edges of a raised bed. Use a trowel or shovel to lift the cut pieces of grass and soil and add them to a compost pile.

CHAPTER THREE

PLANTING AND TENDING

With the big job of building beds behind you, the fun part of gardening awaits. Planting, watching the young plants sprout and grow, watering and feeding them, and enjoying the harvest are to come! Along with planting and harvesting are a few tasks you may enjoy less: mulching, weeding, and dealing with pest problems. But the monotonous chores will be only a small part of the picture in a well-managed raised-bed garden.

PLANTING HOW-TO

PLANTING A RAISED BED is similar to planting a regular garden, but easier, because the soil is always loose and easy to work with. You'll be planting a combination of seeds and transplants. Some crops are easy to grow directly from seed, but for others it's best to begin with transplants that have been grown indoors or in a greenhouse for the first 6 to 8 weeks of life (see facing page).

Some gardeners make a detailed plan on paper before they start planting. Others make decisions more spontaneously about what to plant where. Whichever approach you take, it's wise to decide right from the start how *intensively* you want to plant your garden; that means thinking about how much space to leave between individual plants and groups or rows of plants.

The number of plants that will fit in a typical 4-foot × 6-foot or 4-foot × 8-foot raised bed varies depending on the crop and on your gardening strategy. Some crops naturally grow larger than others — a tomato plant grows much bigger than a lettuce plant, for example, so you'd plant a lot fewer tomato plants in a bed than you would lettuce. Strategy matters, too: If you plan to devote lots of time and energy to your garden all season long, you can squeeze more plants into a bed and succeed. But if you know you have limited time, it's better to space plants farther apart. It's logical: the soil is the reservoir of nutrients and water for crops. Plants that are widely spaced have more soil volume per plant from which to draw water and nutrients, so they will rely less on input from you.

Other factors affect spacing choices, too, but crop size and gardening strategy are the ones to consider first. So, how *do* you decide how many plants to put in each of your raised beds? In other words, how far apart should you space seeds or seedlings at planting time?

Seeds or Transplants?

Some raised-bed crops do best from seed because their roots don't like to be disturbed. With other crops, there's a big advantage to starting seeds indoors, either to protect the small seedlings from pests or to get a head start with crops that take a long time to reach maturity. Here are some lists of crops to start from seed, crops to plant as transplants, and crops that do well either way:

Best grown from seed

- Peas
- Beans
- Radishes and turnips
- Carrots
- Lettuce, spinach, arugula, and other leafy greens

Best grown from transplants

- Tomatoes
- Peppers
- Eggplant
- Broccoli
- Brussels sprouts
- Cabbage

Crops to start either way

- Beets
- Kale and mustard
- Chard
- Sweet corn
- Cucumbers
- Squash and melons

Figuring Out the Spacing

It's easy to find recommendations about vegetable crop spacing on seed packets, in catalogs, in books, online, or from gardening friends. But you'll soon discover that the recommendations vary! Some may call for standard row planting, some for intensive gardening, and others for spacing somewhere in between.

STANDARD SPACING

Standard row spacing allows for plenty of open space between one row of crop plants and the neighboring row. An example of standard spacing for carrots might be "Sow seeds 2 inches apart in rows 30 inches apart. Thin the seedlings to 4 inches apart." That open space provides access for people to walk or tractor wheels to drive between the rows of plants (for tasks such as weeding and applying fertilizer). But when you garden in raised beds, you won't be walking or driving a tractor between the rows! Instead, you can plan for crop rows to be closer together.

And what about the recommendation to sow carrot seeds 2 inches apart and then thin them to 4 inches apart? This type of recommendation applies most to seeds that are planted on a large scale, whether by machine or by hand. It is based on the assumption that a certain percentage of seeds won't germinate, perhaps because they got buried too deeply, didn't get covered up at all, or were eaten by birds. Spacing seeds closely gives the farmer some assurance that enough seedlings will germinate to produce a good yield. If too many seedlings germinate, thinning might be required: pulling out or cutting off excess seedlings to leave just one seedling every 4 inches along the row.

Seed Quality

The fine print on a seed packet should include a germination rate (that is, an estimate of what percentage of the seeds will germinate). Seed companies continually test samples of the seeds they sell to ensure that the seeds are still viable and that the minimum germination percentage meets government standards. The minimum percentage varies by crop. For example, the minimum germination percentage required for pepper seeds is 55 percent, but for peas and lettuce, it's 80 percent. Seed from reputable companies often has a higher germination rate than the minimum standard. But if you buy inexpensive seed, you may find that the germination rate is not as reliable. Also, if seed has aged or been kept in unfavorable conditions (hot and/or humid), the germination rate may be lower than the rate shown on the package.

Before you plant old seeds or seeds of questionable quality in your garden, run a germination test. Sprout 10 seeds between pieces of moist paper towels, or plant them in moist potting mix in a small cup. Multiply the number of healthy seedlings produced by 10 to figure out the germination rate. For example, if 8 of the 10 seeds sprout, the germination rate is 80 percent.

But when you're sowing seeds on a limited scale in the ideal conditions of a raised bed, you can be confident that your germination percentage will be high. So you may want to sow seeds at the final desired spacing. Once the stand of seedlings has poked through the soil, you can skip the task of thinning;

you may, however, need to resow to fill the occasional gap where a seed didn't germinate.

INTENSIVE SPACING

In an intensive garden, plants are arranged to completely cover the bed surface. A gardener choosing intensive spacing might sow carrot seeds 3 inches apart in the row and sow several rows 3 inches apart. As the plants grow, they will eventually form a forestlike cover over the surface of the bed, with no soil showing through at all.

This method offers the advantage of higher yields, plus less need for weeding because the crops themselves shade out any weeds that sprout among them. The soil in the intensively planted plot will fill up completely with crop roots. Plants that are intensively managed need soil that is rich in nutrients and organic matter, and possibly supplemental fertilizer, throughout the season. The continuous covering of foliage does help keep the soil cooler and moister than if it were bare, but the intensive infiltration of roots pumps lots of moisture out of the soil. So watering will be important during any period without adequate rain — and adequate in this case may be more than the standard rule of thumb of 1 inch of rain per week.

Because of the wonderful soil and the gardener's willingness to pamper the plants, it's possible to pack a bed with plants and end up with excellent yield. For example, an intensively planted 4-foot × 8-foot raised bed of carrots might yield as much as 100 pounds of carrots!

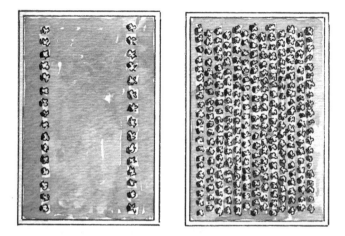

STANDARD ROW SPACING (above left) in a raised bed leaves much more open space than is needed, but intensive spacing (above right) may be too crowded if your soil is less than ideal. For a first-rate garden, the best choice could be something in between, such as the bed below.

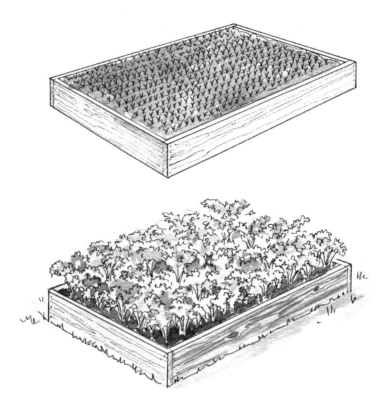

INDIVIDUAL ROWS OF CARROT SEEDLINGS are separate at first in an intensive planting (top), but as the plants grow the foliage expands to create a dense green covering across the entire bed (bottom).

IN-BETWEEN SPACING

Are there choices other than standard row spacing and intensive spacing? Sure there are. In fact, there are almost infinite choices. You could space crop rows more tightly than standard spacing (for example, 18 or 12 inches apart) but not as tightly as an intensively managed bed. This intermediate approach offers the advantage of better air circulation around the plants, because some open space between rows will remain even as the plants mature. That's helpful, especially in humid climates, because air circulation helps prevent disease problems.

Figuring out a planting plan for a raised bed is one of the most fun and creative opportunities in gardening. You may make some choices that don't work out well, but you'll learn from those (especially if you keep a raised-bed garden journal), and you'll surely have some exciting successes, too. Remember to keep an optimistic and experimental attitude! Some gardeners are experimenting with spacing plants extra-far apart — spacing eggplants 5 feet apart, for example. They mulch the rest of the soil surface well, and they find that the eggplants grow much larger than they usually do (the plants do require some staking) and the yields are much higher than traditional expectations. This kind of experimentation is one of the fascinations of working with living organisms that respond to their environment. As you gain experience, you'll learn to "read" your plants' reactions by factors such as their leaf color, size, and appearance; how fast they're growing; and how quickly they start developing flowers.

The Planting Puzzle

Figuring out a planting plan is like solving a puzzle. It involves some math, some reasoned consideration of the factors that affect plant growth, some knowledge of your soil, and some intuition.

As you make a planting plan, assign a rating of 1 to 5 to each of your answers to these questions:

- How fertile is my soil? 1 = poor, 5 = excellent
- How well does my soil hold water and/or how much am I willing to take time to water? 1 = very little, 5 = abundant
- What's the weather like during my growing season? 1 = hot and dry, 5 = moderate and moist
- What about insect pests and diseases in my area? 1 = lots of potential problems, 5 = usually very few

If you end up with a score of 15 or greater, you may do very well with intensive planting. If the score is lower, you'll be most likely to succeed if you take a less-than-intensive approach to planting. And you can always experiment with an intensive test planting of one small bed or a portion of a bed. You may discover that you rated your garden more severely than you needed to.

Sowing Seeds

Sowing seeds is a simple form of garden artistry, and with a little experimentation, you'll discover the seed-sowing tricks you like best. The basic choices are sowing in furrows, sowing in wide bands (or broadcasting), and sowing in individual planting holes. Whichever method you choose, you can buy or improvise tools to aid in the task.

Here's some sound general advice: sow early and often. Sow early because it's impossible to predict the weather. Sow early, and you'll be happily rewarded with an early crop if the weather is warmer than average. Sow often (in small quantities) for two reasons: first, making several small sowings of a crop is insurance against a spell of bad weather. For example, if you sow an entire packet of lettuce seed and a period of heavy rain follows, all that seed may be washed away. But if you split up the packet into four or more weekly seedings, you would lose only a quarter of the packet to that spell of heavy rain. Second, sowing small quantities weekly or every 2 weeks spreads out the harvest. Planting too much seed at once leads to a glut of produce you won't be able to keep up with.

Before you sow, check the seed packet for the proper seed depth. Generally, the smaller the seed, the more shallowly it's planted. Also remember to add some fungal inoculant to the soil (or rhizobacteria for peas and beans) as you plant, especially in new garden beds.

SOWING IN HOLES

Dibble planting works well for large seeds such as peas and beans. A dibble is a tool used to make holes in the soil. Your finger can be a dibble, or you can use a small stick or the end of a tool handle. If you use a long-handled tool, you can stand up straight while making the holes rather than bending over or kneeling. To use as a depth guide, mark lines on your dibble at $\frac{1}{2}$ inch, 1 inch, and 2 inches. Simply poke a hole of the correct depth at each spot where you want to plant a seed. Drop a seed (or two for insurance) into each hole, then water the seeded row, and the soil will naturally fill in the holes.

SOWING IN FURROWS

Use the corner of a hoe or a trowel blade to "plow" open a furrow, or lay a long-handled tool along the row and press down gently to form a U-shaped furrow.

Sowing small seeds into a furrow takes patience. Measure out roughly the amount of seed you'll need for the length of the furrow. You can then put the seeds into a small dish or box; add some sand or dry, sifted compost; and mix. You may find it easier to sow a mixture like this evenly along the furrow.

Some gardeners dribble out seeds between the thumb and forefinger. Others put seeds into a handheld seed dispenser, or just a piece of folded paper, and tap it lightly to make seeds drop out one by one.

Next, with your fingers, gently pinch the soil along the sides of the furrow back into place. Or use more sifted compost or commercial seed-starting mix to cover over the furrows. (Compost and seed-starting mix may be less likely to crust over than plain soil.) Water gently.

BROADCASTING

Another approach to planting is to spread seeds across the entire surface of the planting area. This works well for crops such as lettuce, spinach, baby kale, and arugula, which you'll harvest by cutting bunches of leaves with scissors.

To prepare for broadcasting, use your hand or the edge of a piece of scrap wood to smooth out the soil surface. Then calculate approximately how much seed you want to sow in that area, count or measure out the seeds, and sprinkle them over the soil surface. Use the flat of your hand to gently press the seeds into contact with the soil. Cover the seeds with sifted compost or a purchased seed-starting mix. Then spread a light mulch of grass clippings or straw, just enough to lightly shade the soil surface. Water very gently after sowing.

FOLLOWING UP

Some seeds germinate within 24 hours, but others take several days. Carrot seedlings may take up to 2 weeks to emerge from the soil. Germinating seeds are vulnerable; if the soil dries out, seedlings may die or become stunted. Check newly seeded areas daily, and apply water as often as needed, which could be daily or even twice a day during hot summer weather. Use a watering can with a fine rose head, one with many tiny holes that delivers water gently and evenly. Or water with a handheld hose, using a nozzle set to a mist or shower setting. You don't need to water new seedlings too deeply — your goal is not to soak the soil, but to keep the top inch or two consistently moist as the seeds send out their first roots and shoots.

Setting Out Transplants

When it comes to transplants, the more locally grown they are, the better. Most vegetable and flower bedding plants sold at home centers and even some garden centers have been grown in huge commercial greenhouses and shipped long distances. The plants are growing in soilless mix and entirely dependent on liquid chemical fertilizer for nutrition. They're not the best prepared for life in an organic garden. If you can, seek out a local grower who uses a compost-based growing mix and has cared for the plants well, including hardening them off — a process of gradually exposing the tender young plants to outdoor conditions. Transplants that aren't hardened off may suffer transplant shock when set out in the garden, and that can set back their growth by 2 weeks or more.

You can also try growing seedlings yourself in containers indoors. It's a fun project, and a great way to have exactly the choice of varieties you want to grow.

Planting transplants is a cinch. Simply measure out where each plant should go, based on your planting plan or your on-the-spot spacing decisions. With a trowel, dig a hole deep enough for the rootball. If you wish, add some compost to the bottom of the planting hole. Then pour in a couple of cups of water. Set the plant in place and gently but firmly mold the soil over the rootball and up to the stem. Use your finger to make a shallow moat a few inches away from the plant stem. Then water again. The plant will transition best when the soil is very moist.

For any plant that has a bare central stem, such as peppers or broccoli, you can position the rootball an inch or so deeper than the soil surface to get the plants off to an even better start. This doesn't work well for plants that sprout out from a central growing point, such as lettuce or squash.

Interplanting

Interplanting is a serious-sounding term for a simple concept. It simply means planting a variety of kinds of plants in and among each other. Interplanting is a helpful technique because it makes optimal use of space. For example, once you set out broccoli plants in a bed, you can put lettuce transplants in the open gaps between the broccoli. Within a month, the lettuce will be ready to harvest, and after that the broccoli plants will fill all the gaps with their expanding foliage.

Interplanting with certain plants is reputed to help repel pests. For example, sowing radish seeds around young cucumber or squash plants may help repel cucumber beetles.

Flowering annuals are always a great choice for interplanting. They add color and variety that will increase your gardening pleasure, and many of them, such as alyssum and calendulas, attract beneficial insects that actually prey on caterpillars and other insect pests that eat vegetable crops.

Plant This with That

Choosing crops to interplant is a good exercise in creativity and logic. Consider both the type of top growth and the type of root growth of your plant companions. A deep-rooted crop is a good neighbor for a shallow-rooted crop, for example, because they'll draw nutrients from different parts of the soil. And a tall bushy crop can be a good companion for a short crop that benefits from some afternoon shade in hot weather. Here are a few well-known interplanting schemes:

- Basil around tomatoes
- Onions and cabbage
- Spinach or arugula in the shade of tomatoes or trellised cucumbers
- Corn and winter squash
- Nasturtiums (pest repellents) with squash
- Marigolds (pest repellents) with beans
- Beans and potatoes

POSSIBILITIES FOR INTERPLANTING allow for lots of creative variations. Try combining collards, basil, marigolds, and Swiss chard to fill a bed. Beets and tomatoes make good companions, too. When the early planting of beets is harvested, the interplanted tomatoes will continue to expand up and out, filling the spaces where the beets were growing.

WATERING

HAVE YOU EVER HAD a potted plant unexpectedly die, and then discovered that the soil in the pot was bone-dry? It's all too easy to let potted plants dry out. Raised beds aren't as vulnerable to drying out as container gardens are, but they do lose moisture more quickly than an in-ground garden. Neglecting to water enough is a common mistake that raised-bed gardeners make.

Once you've begun planting, pay close attention to the water status of your garden. How can you tell when your raised-bed garden needs water? One strategy is to measure rainfall. Buy a rain gauge, which consists of a plastic reservoir calibrated in inches for easy reading (available from garden suppliers and home center), and set it up in or near your garden. Check the gauge every time it rains and keep records. A broad rule of thumb is that gardens need 1 inch of water per week. Light, sandy soils may need even more water than that because water drains through them more quickly. Hot conditions can increase the need for water, and the density of planting has an effect, too.

Another way is to touch the soil and see whether it feels moist. Soil dries out from the surface down, so you want to investigate the root zone, not just the soil surface. Dig a little hole and observe the top few inches of soil. If the entire top inch of the soil is dry, it's time to water.

How much water should you apply? It's best to water deeply to encourage roots to grow deeply. In general, apply at least 1 inch of water across the entire surface of the bed. That translates to 5 pints per square foot of garden area. Thus, a

100-square-foot bed needs 500 pints. There are 8 pints in a gallon, which means you'll need to apply about 62 gallons to the bed. More than you expected? It's a lot of water! But don't set up a bucket brigade! It's best to apply water slowly and steadily, not by pouring bucketfuls all at once. You can water by hand or with some type of irrigation system.

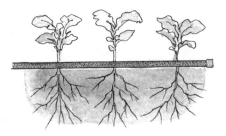

WATER FROM A SOAKER HOSE or drip fitting gently soaks into the soil both vertically (top) and laterally (bottom) to moisten the entire root zone.

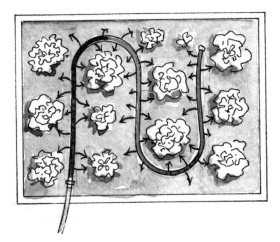

Figuring Flow Rate

Start by figuring out the rate at which your hose or irrigation setup delivers water. To see how fast water flows from an outdoor faucet, hook up a hose, attach a nozzle (the "gentle shower" setting is usually good for watering plants), and put the nozzle in a 5-gallon bucket. Turn on the hose to deliver water at the desired force — not too weak, not too strong. Time

A LOW-TECH VERSION of drip irrigation is a set of homemade watering reservoirs: plastic milk jugs or water bottles sunk into the soil. Use a small nail to poke many small holes into each jug, bury it up to the top, and use a watering can or a hose to fill it. The water will be absorbed slowly and spread through the soil.

how long it takes to fill the bucket. If it takes 2 minutes, then the flow rate is 2½ gallons per minute. Divide 62 gallons by 2½, and you'll find that it takes approximately 25 minutes of watering to deliver 1 inch of water to that 100-square-foot bed.

As you calculate how long you need to water, factor in natural rainfall. If ½ inch of rain fell during the week, then you need to supplement your garden with only ½ inch of water, or about 12 minutes of watering.

How and When to Water

Watering your garden by hand can be a lovely meditative exercise. Morning is an ideal time to water, when conditions are cool and less water will be lost to evaporation. Aim to water the ground surface rather than the foliage. Start out gently, because when the soil surface or surface mulch is dry, it may repel water at first, resulting in water running off in little streams rather than soaking in evenly. As the surface layer becomes wet, the soil will absorb water more quickly. Keep in mind that you don't have to water your entire garden all at once, either. For example, you might choose to water a 20-square-foot area for 5 minutes one morning, the adjacent 20-square-foot section the following morning, and so on.

One of the most time- and water-efficient ways to care for your raised beds is to use soaker hoses or a drip irrigation system. Buying the equipment and setting it up requires an investment of dollars and time, but once in place a soaker hose or drip irrigation system is the ideal way to water. For more on setting up a watering system, see page 78.

Sprinkler Pros and Cons

If you don't have the time or patience to water by hand, you can use a sprinkler instead, but there are drawbacks. The spray from a sprinkler will leave the foliage thoroughly wet, and wet foliage is more susceptible to infection by disease organisms. Also, most sprinklers deliver water in an uneven pattern, so some parts of a bed will be soaked while other parts are barely wetted. Also, because sprinklers shoot water out into the air, a portion of the water will evaporate before it ever reaches the soil.

A small sprinkler can work well for watering newly seeded areas, if it has a mist setting. Run the sprinkler for a short period (as little as 10 minutes) daily to ensure the seeded area never dries out, which will help to ensure quick, even germination.

If you plan to use a sprinkler to thoroughly water a bed of growing plants, first check the delivery rate and pattern of your sprinkler. Set it up in the raised bed and set our several shallow empty cans (cat food cans work well) across the bed. Turn on the sprinkler for a defined interval, such as 20 minutes. Then turn off the sprinkler and check each can. You may be surprised to find that some cans are full to overflowing while others are only half full. If the sprinkler pattern is too uneven, the sprinkler probably isn't worth using. If only one or two cans are lacking in water, though, you can use the sprinkler, then follow up by hand-watering the spots that the sprinkler spray isn't covering well.

MULCHING AND FEEDING

MULCHING YOUR GARDEN is another task you'll need to tend to shortly after planting. It's easy to do, and mulch offers many benefits:

- Smothers weed seedlings
- Blocks evaporation, which keeps the soil moist (and that's good for soil microbes)
- Is an additional food source for the life in the soil
- Moderates soil temperature
- Protects the soil from erosion during heavy rain
- Prevents soil from spattering up onto foliage during rain or watering, which can help prevent diseases

Two of the most common mulches for vegetable beds are shredded leaves and grass clippings. Grass clippings are easily available during the growing season, from your own lawn or from nearby lawns (but be sure that those lawns haven't been treated with pesticides or herbicides).

To have a supply of shredded leaves requires planning. In the fall, you can set up a leaf corral made of garden fencing or snow fencing attached to a few sturdy stakes. Dump leaves into the corral and tamp them down throughout the fall, then cover the corral with a tarp for the winter. Or you can simply load leaves into large plastic trash bags and store them in a pile or in a garden shed for the winter. If you don't have a shredder, run a lawn mower over fallen leaves to chop them up roughly.

Other mulches that work well include straw, hay (although hay may contain lots of seeds that could become future weeds), and pine needles. Spread mulch about 1 inch thick, and leave a little open space between the mulch and the seeded rows or individual plant stems.

Mulch offers the greatest benefit early in the season. As your crops grow, their foliage takes over some of the duties of mulch, shading the soil surface and stifling weed competition.

Raised beds filled with rich soil mix may have enough of a storehouse of nutrients to feed crops all season long. Watch your crops for clues about whether fertilizer is needed. If the rate of growth begins to slow or foliage color changes, that could be a sign that your crops need a boost. Compost is always an option for feeding your crops, if you have enough of it. If you don't have enough, you'll need to buy a commercial product.

Choices of commercial fertilizers abound, but it can be hard to tell which products are suitable for organic gardens. The words "natural" and even "organic" on a fertilizer label aren't necessarily a guarantee that a fertilizer is free of synthetic components. Instead, look for products with the logo of the Organic Materials Review Institute (OMRI) on the label or ask for recommendations from a knowledgeable staff person at a local garden center.

It's easy to apply dry fertilizers by side-dressing — spreading the fertilizer on the soil surface alongside the plants. But in cool conditions, you may get better results from applying a liquid fertilizer such as liquid seaweed directly to the leaves.

Another way to build fertility is to plant cover crops. This is also one way to resolve a weed problem. (See page 68 for more about cover crops.)

DEALING WITH WEEDS, PESTS, AND DISEASES

PROBLEMS WILL BE FEW in a raised-bed garden as long as you keep up with watering regularly and feeding the soil. But any garden can suffer an outbreak of a pest or a disease, and weed competition can build up over the seasons. Here's some basic advice on how to cope with weed, pest, and disease problems.

Outwitting Weeds

Weeds may not be much of a problem in a new raised-bed garden, especially if you use a purchased soil mix or bagged commercial compost. And intensive planting helps prevent weed problems because the crop plants quickly form a cover that prevents weed seed germination.

Over time, though, weeds have a way of infiltrating garden beds. Happily, pulling weeds in a raised bed is often almost effortless because the soil is so loose — the weeds slip right out, roots and all.

Germinating weed seeds. If one of your raised beds seems weedier than the other, try to outwit the weeds by tricking the weed seeds into germinating before you plant your crop. About a week before you plan to plant, water the bed well; then check it daily and keep the surface moist. This treatment will prompt most of the weed seeds near the surface of the soil to sprout. Just after the weed seedlings emerge, you can destroy them. Use a weeding tool such as a circle hoe or hula hoe designed for cutting just below the soil surface to slice through the weed seedling stems. Do this in the morning on a sunny day so that the weed seedlings will dry up and die before midafternoon. After that, disturb the soil as little as possible when you sow your seeds, and your crop will sprout and grow with little weed competition.

Planting cover crops. Another way to knock back a weed problem is to plant a cover crop either before or after your main crop. The main purpose of a cover crop, as you might guess, is to cover the soil surface. It's a living version of mulch, and it serves many of the same purposes. Common cover crops for gardens include oats, rye, and buckwheat. These crops grow densely, and they're good at shading out any weeds that try to compete with them.

Which cover crop to grow depends primarily on the time of year. Oats are a good choice for spring, and buckwheat is a fast-growing summer crop. Winter rye is perfect for sowing in late summer or early fall because it grows better in cold temperatures than other cover crops do, and it will survive over winter and continue growing the following spring.

Cover-crop seed is easy to sow, and the crops are trouble-free. It is important, however, to cut down a cover crop before it goes to seed. Otherwise, the cover crop plants will drop seeds all over your garden, and the seeds may germinate when you don't want them to — and then you have a new weed problem! Cover crops offer another great benefit besides suppressing weeds: lots and lots of organic matter, which you can gently dig into the top few inches of the soil to enrich it. Or, after you've cut the cover crop, leave the "greens" to dry down on the soil surface as a mulch, and simply pull the mulch back out of the way when you're ready to plant. (For detailed information on how to plant and manage cover crops, see Resources, page 87.)

Raised-Bed Recordkeeping

If you like to keep a journal or diary, you'll probably enjoy keeping a garden journal, too. Write about everything and anything related to your garden, but especially note the "how I did it" details: describe your seed-sowing methods, transplanting techniques, weeding tricks, and watering routines. And be sure to keep track of what you planted when by making a planting map right in your journal.

For those who don't want to keep a full-fledged journal, try one of these tricks:

- **Make daily notes on a large wall calendar.** Include sowing dates, germination dates, watering dates (and how much water applied), and date of first and last harvest for each crop.

- **Use your computer or handheld device.** You can download garden recordkeeping software, or you can make your own template.

- **Keep notes on a set of 5 × 7 cards.** Use one card for each crop you grow, and store the cards in a sturdy plastic box with a hinged lid. Take the box to the garden and jot notes about each crop as you work.

Keep your recordkeeping aspirations simple. The more requirements you set for yourself, the more likely you are to fall behind, and that's discouraging. Even if you record only the planting date, the date first fruit appears, the date of the first harvest, and the date of the last harvest, that's a good start!

Managing Pests and Diseases

Every garden will have some problems with pests and diseases, and raised-bed gardens are no exception. Some common signs of pest or disease problems are holes in the leaves or brown, wilted leaves at the base of a plant. These signs are distressing, but chances are that most of what you plant will produce and grow well.

If you do discover a pest problem in your garden, the first step is to sleuth out the specific cause. You can do that by comparing damage symptoms or insects (if you spot them, usually on the underside of leaves) to the photos in a pest and disease identification guide; by asking a knowledgeable gardening friend what's causing the problem; or by taking a sample of the damaged plant parts and/or any bugs, beetles, caterpillars, and the like you find on or near the suffering plants to your local Cooperative Extension Service for expert identification.

Keep in mind that one of the best ways to minimize plant problems is to build healthy soil. Plants that are growing vigorously are less susceptible to attack by many pests and disease organisms, and microbes in a healthy soil actually produce substances to help protect plants against disease.

Preventing problems with row covers. Another strategy for preventing many potential pest problems is to cover beds with row covers. Row covers are pieces of lightweight synthetic fabric that allow air and water to pass through, but not insect pests. You can drape row covers directly over plants or rest them on wire or plastic hoops (as shown on page 71). It's important to seal the edges of the covers at the soil surface by weighing

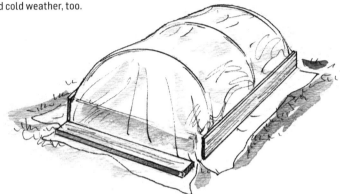

ROW COVERS are easy to put in place over a raised bed. The lightweight cover helps prevent a wide range of pest problems and offer plants a little protection from wind and cold weather, too.

them down with rocks, boards, or soil so that pests can't crawl underneath.

Fighting slugs. Slugs are a common pest that can't be excluded with row covers. These soft-bodied creatures (which are mollusks, as are shellfish) can burrow through the surface soil and come up on the inside of a row cover tunnel. And slugs love the protected environment under a tunnel. They also do well in beds that are mulched, because the mulch helps keep the soil moist.

Slugs are susceptible to commercial slug baits, but choose carefully. Some baits are made from synthetic materials. A good choice is an iron phosphate bait, such as Sluggo, which is not harmful to people or pets but is toxic to slugs.

You can also handpick slugs off plants (they're active in the early morning or at night) and drop them into a can of soapy water. Or fasten a strip of copper all around the frame of your raised bed. Slugs can't cross a copper barrier, so it will permanently stop them.

Slugs have plenty of natural predators, so as your garden matures and develops a native population of predators such as ground beetles, any slug problem you have may decrease all on its own.

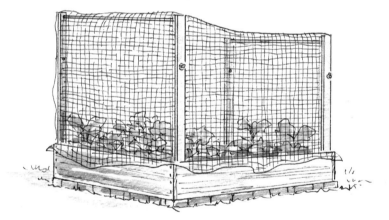

A PEST FENCE around a raised bed doesn't have to be heavy-duty. Plastic netting held tightly in place against wooden uprights will deter most four-footed pests. Simply unscrew the wingnut and open the fence to tend the bed.

Preventing animal damage. The most troublesome pests for many vegetable gardeners are those with four feet, such as deer, woodchucks, and rabbits. Covering beds with row covers may be enough to prevent damage from some animals, but woodchucks and deer have been known to push or tear right through row covers to reach the treats underneath. You can cage a bed by stretching chicken wire over plastic or wire hoops. Or make a barrier with netting, such as the one shown on page 72.

You can use smelly repellents, such as strong-smelling deodorant soap or a garlic spray around the perimeter of your raised beds. These may stop pests for a while, but animals sometimes learn to ignore a repellent. To increase effectiveness, try switching the type of repellent every few weeks.

There are also commercial repellent devices that use motion sensors to activate a bright light or a spray of water when pests approach the garden. You can find these at garden centers or through online garden suppliers.

CHAPTER FOUR

ACCESSORIZING YOUR BED

Creating raised beds is a satisfying project all on its own. To get the best from your beds, though, you may want to add a set of support hoops for row covers or netting, a watering system, and a variety of trellises. These accessories will help you produce more food with less work, prevent pest damage, and extend the growing season. You can also accessorize your bed with artistic touches for the fun of it, including flowers, garden artwork, or a place to sit.

SETTING UP A SUPPORT SYSTEM

A framework of plastic pipes or flexible metal hoop supports straddling a raised bed is handy for supporting shade cloth for hot-climate growing. A frame also works well for draping netting over a bed to keep out animal pests or to support floating row covers or plastic sheeting to protect crops from cold conditions and extend the growing season.

You can simply stick the ends of a ½-inch-diameter plastic pipe (available from home centers) into the soil to create semicircular hoops, but for a more secure frame, it works well to install anchors on the inside of the frame. Wire hoops (available from farm and garden suppliers) also work well when inserted directly into the soil.

HOOPS FASHIONED FROM sections of plastic pipe, spaced 4 to 5 feet apart, can support various coverings to protect your crops from pests and extreme weather.

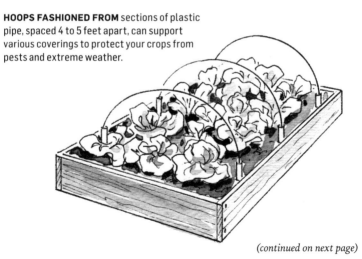

(continued on next page)

MATERIALS

- ½-inch-diameter plastic pipe or flexible metal hoop supports
- Rigid 1-inch-diameter pipe
- Tube straps
- Rocks, boards, or bags filled with soil for use as anchors

TOOLS

- Hacksaw
- Screwdriver or portable drill

1. For the anchors, cut sections of the 1-inch-diameter pipe into lengths about equal to the height of the walls of your bed.

SECTIONS OF TUBING FASTENED to the raised-bed frame with tube straps will hold hoop supports securely in place.

2. Install tube straps to fasten the pipes to the frame wall.

3. Once the anchors are in place, cut the $1/2$-inch-diameter plastic pipe into sections of equal length. For a 4-foot-wide bed, cut hoops about 7 feet long (or longer if you want to grow taller crops in the bed).

4. Feed the ends of the hoops into the anchor posts, and then spread the covering of choice over the hoops. Anchor the covers.

If you want to add a support system to an existing bed that's already filled with soil, you can strap the anchor pipes to the outside of the frame boards rather than the inside. Or you can use pieces of rebar as anchors. You'll need pieces about 18 inches long. Drive them into the soil so that a section about 6 inches long sticks up above the top of the frame. The ends of the hoops will slip right over the rebar. When the hoops aren't in place, the exposed rebar can be a hazard; you could scratch your hands or arms on it while tending your plants. To avoid this, make slits in old tennis balls and slip a ball over each piece of rebar. Or paint the exposed rebar a bright color so you'll be sure to notice and avoid it.

INSTALLING A WATERING SYSTEM

BECAUSE RAISED BEDS ARE PRONE to drying out, it's well worth the time and expense to install soaker hoses or a drip irrigation line. These systems deliver water directly to the soil, and there's minimal run-off or evaporation. Foliage stays dry, which lessens the risk of disease problems.

Soaker hoses. Soaker hoses slowly weep drops of water through small pores all over the surface of the hose. Soaker hoses are the easiest and least expensive choice for a watering system. Simply lay out the soaker hose on the surface of the bed. Use U-shaped wire pins to hold the hose in place if it seems to have a mind of its own. Once the soaker hose is in place, spread a layer of straw or other coarse mulch over it. This will help hold moisture in the soil longer by reducing

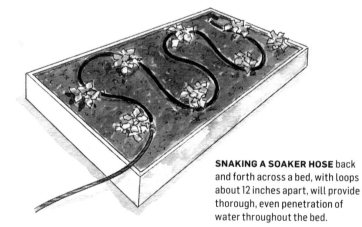

SNAKING A SOAKER HOSE back and forth across a bed, with loops about 12 inches apart, will provide thorough, even penetration of water throughout the bed.

evaporation from the soil surface. Or you can bury hoses in the soil itself, up to 4 inches deep.

The amount of water delivered by a soaker hose varies depending on the water pressure from the source and the brand of soaker hose, so it's a good idea to run a test to see how long it takes for your soaker hose setup to wet the soil. To do this, make sure the pressure regulator is in place and then turn on the water. About 45 minutes later, dig down into the soil with a trowel. The soil should be moist at least 6 inches deep. If it's not, leave the water on and recheck again about 10 minutes later. Keep checking until the soil is moist 6 inches deep. Checking your system this way the first few times you use it will give you a good idea of how long it takes to provide a thorough watering. When you know how long it takes to water to a depth of 6 inches, simply turn on the hose, set a timer to remind yourself, and turn off the hose when the timer dings. Or use a watering hose timer (available from garden centers and home centers), which will automatically turn off the water after the allotted time.

It's best to set up a separate soaker hose for each bed, because if water travels through more than 100 feet of soaker hose, the pressure drop at the end of the hose may be so great that the soil in that area won't receive much water.

Drip irrigation. A drip irrigation system may consist of plastic tubes or a hose with built-in "drippers" (fittings that release water), or you may find a system that allows you to insert the drippers into the hose at the desired positions. If you are installing emitters yourself, space the emitters 6 to 12 inches

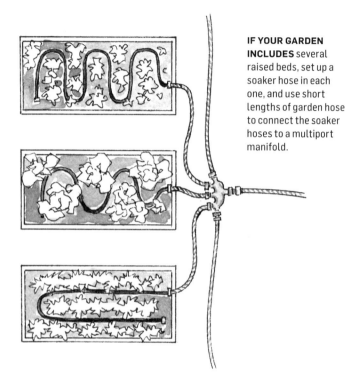

IF YOUR GARDEN INCLUDES several raised beds, set up a soaker hose in each one, and use short lengths of garden hose to connect the soaker hoses to a multiport manifold.

apart. Keep in mind that a drip irrigation hose releases water only through the emitters, not from its entire surface the way a soaker hose does.

If you decide to use drip irrigation, you may find it convenient to use a kit. Drip irrigation kits often include a pressure regulator and angle couplings to allow the lines to change directions.

SENDING YOUR GARDEN INTO SPACE

SINCE SPACE IS OFTEN AT A PREMIUM in raised beds, make use of the vertical space above your beds, too, by training plants on trellises. Any type of trellis that works in a standard garden bed should also serve the purpose in a raised bed. The thing to keep in mind is how loose and light the soil in a raised bed is. Because of that, take extra care to anchor trellises. Once you set a trellis in place, hammer in 18-inch-long pieces of rebar at the base of the trellis and then lash the trellis tightly to the rebar.

TEPEE-STYLE TRELLISES are good for raised beds because they tend to be more self-supporting than straight-up-and-down trellises.

HOW TO BUILD A STURDY VERTICAL TRELLIS

If you'd like to make a vertical trellis along one edge of a bed for tomatoes or cucumbers, use tall metal fence posts for the end poles of the trellis.

MATERIALS

- 2 metal fence posts, 8 feet tall
- 2×4 timber, cut to appropriate length
- 2 pieces of utility wire, about 12 inches long, plus additional wire for stringing the trellis
- 2-inch galvanized wood screws (optional)

TOOLS

- 1-pound sledge or fence-post driver
- Tape measure
- Handsaw or circular saw
- Power drill

1. Use the sledge to pound one post into each end of the bed, sinking each post at least 8 inches into the undisturbed soil below the shallow raised bed.

2. Use the tape measure to measure the distance between the top of the posts, and cut a 2 × 4 to that length.

3. Use the saw to cut a notch in each end of the 2 × 4. Then use the power drill to drill one hole through the timber at each end, a few inches in from the end. Feed a long piece of sturdy wire through each of the holes.

4. Wedge the 2 × 4 between the posts, catching the wedge on the posts' protruding tongues. Use the wires to fasten the 2 × 4 to the posts.

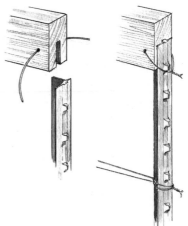

5. Run a few courses of wire between the posts, with wires spaced about 1 foot apart vertically. Or, if you want to use the trellis for pole beans, install screws at regular intervals along the wooden frame of the bed, leaving about ½ inch of each screw protruding. Run a length of twine from each screw up to the top bar of the trellis.

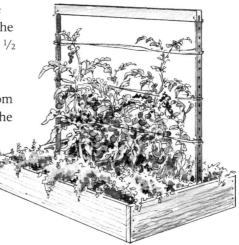

ADDING ARTISTIC TOUCHES

Gardening is a skill, but it's also an art. With your raised beds as frames, you can create beautiful and unique living pictures that combine your vegetables and herbs with flowers, sculpture, and more.

There are good reasons to plant some flowers in every raised bed, even if your primary goal is to raise food crops. Why flowers? The most important reason is that they attract beneficial insects such as lacewings and lady beetles that prey on common pests, including aphids. They're inexpensive, natural pest prevention. Let some flowers go to seed, too, and they'll attract sweet songbirds such as goldfinches. Those finches will eat the seeds, but they'll eat insects and weed seeds, too. Flowers also attract bees and other pollinators to gardens, which is very beneficial for crops such as squash and cucumbers that rely on insects for pollination.

Plus, flowers are a natural pick-me-up for people. What's your reaction when you see a patch of bright zinnias or a cascading sweep of pretty petunias? You smile, right? Right! Flowers will improve the appearance of any garden, and that will add to your sense of success, which will lead you to spend more time in your garden, which will lead to even greater success!

Good choices for adding color or attracting pollinators are sweet alyssum, calendulas, cosmos, marigolds, violas, zinnias, and sunflowers. Plant cascading flowers such as alyssum and nasturtiums along the edges of a bed where they can cascade over the sides. Cluster flowers around the base of a trellis. You can even add perennial herbs such as thyme and rosemary at the corners of your beds, where they'll come back year after year.

It's fun to plan a color scheme for a mixed planting of flowers and vegetables. Purple and pink alyssum look lovely next to purple basil and eggplant or red-hued leaf lettuce. Try white alyssum or violas next to dark green kale or chard, or the reddish foliage of beets.

A TALL RAISED BED OFFERS extra possibilities for cascading foliage and flowers. Squash, oregano, alyssum, and nasturtiums are just a few of the many types of plants that look beautiful spilling out over the sides of a raised bed.

Artwork can add humor or elegance to a garden, too. Some art objects, such as a birdbath or an obelisk-style trellis, can be both useful and artistic. The picture you create in the framework of your raised beds will be your unique garden portrait that will provide you with daily pleasure and plenty of delicious produce. Enjoy it!

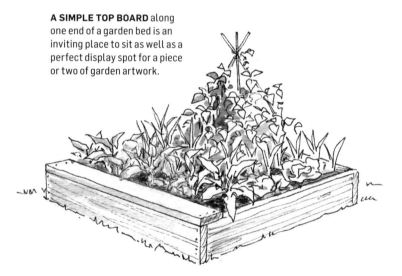

A SIMPLE TOP BOARD along one end of a garden bed is an inviting place to sit as well as a perfect display spot for a piece or two of garden artwork.

RESOURCES

BOOKS

Bradley, Fern Marshall. *Rodale's Vegetable Garden Problem Solver.* Rodale, 2007.

Bradley, Fern Marshall, Barbara W. Ellis, and Deborah L. Martin, eds. *The Organic Gardener's Handbook of Natural Pest and Disease Control.* Rodale, 2009.

Jabbour, Niki. *The Year-Round Vegetable Gardener.* Storey Publishing, 2011.

Karsten, Joel. *Straw Bale Gardens.* Cool Springs Press, 2013.

Littlefield, Cindy, ed. *The Vegetable Gardener's Book of Building Projects.* Storey Publishing, 2010.

Lowenfels, Jeff. *Teaming with Nutrients.* Timber Press, 2013.

Pleasant, Barbara and Deborah L. Martin. *The Complete Compost Gardening Guide.* Storey Publishing, 2008.

Smith, Edward C. *The Vegetable Gardener's Bible, 2nd edition.* Storey Publishing, 2011.

Toensmeier, Eric, and Jonathan Bates. *Paradise Lot.* Chelsea Green, 2013.

WEBSITES

Gardens Alive!
www.gardensalive.com
Soil inoculants, cover crop seed, and a range of other garden products

Mother Earth News
www.motherearthnews.com
Articles and blogs on cover crops, raised beds, organic pest control, and more

Natural Resources Conservation Service
www.nrcs.usda.gov
Information on soil health

Peaceful Valley Farm Supply
www.groworganic.com
Cover crops, soil inoculants, and other supplies

Planet Natural
www.planetnatural.com
Soil inoculants and a range of other garden products

Straw Bale Gardens Blog
http://strawbalegardens.com/blog
Straw bale raised-bed garden techniques

Metric Conversion Chart

WHEN THE MEASUREMENT GIVEN IS	TO CONVERT IT TO	MULTIPLY IT BY
inches	meters	0.0254
feet	meters	0.3048
yards	meters	0.9144
miles	meters	1,609.344
ounces	grams	28.35
pounds	grams	453.5

INDEX

Page numbers in *italic* indicate illustrations; page numbers in **bold** indicate charts.

OTHER STOREY BOOKS YOU WILL ENJOY

Groundbreaking Food Gardens by Niki Jabbour
Featuring a stellar collection of 73 surprising food garden plans from
leading gardeners, this book includes unique themes, innovative layouts,
unusual plant combinations, and space-saving ideas. These illustrated
designs are sure to ignite your own creativity and ingenuity!
272 pages. Paper. ISBN 978-1-61212-061-4.

Homegrown Herbs by Tammi Hartung
This step-by-step primer for gardeners of any level has complete
information on growing and using over 100 herbs for beauty, flavor, and
health. With rich photography and in-depth guidance on seed selection,
planting and maintenance, harvest, and more, this book will introduce
herbs into your life.
256 pages. Paper. ISBN 978-1-60342-703-6.

The Vegetable Gardener's Bible, 2nd Edition
by Edward C. Smith
The 10th anniversary edition of the best-selling vegetable gardening
classic features Ed Smith's time-tested W-O-R-D system for growing an
abundance of organic vegetables, fruits, and herbs in your own backyard.
352 pages. Paper. ISBN 978-1-60342-475-2.
Hardcover. ISBN 978-1-60342-476-9.

The Year-Round Vegetable Gardener by Niki Jabbour
Learn how to grow your own food 365 days a year, no matter where you
live! You'll learn how to select the best varieties for each season, master
the art of succession planting, and make inexpensive protective structures
that keep vegetables viable and delicious through the colder months.
256 pages. Paper. ISBN 978-1-60342-568-1.
Hardcover. ISBN 978-1-60342-992-4.

These and other books from Storey Publishing are available
wherever quality books are sold or by calling 1-800-441-5700.
Visit us at *www.storey.com* or sign up for our newsletter
at *www.storey.com/signup*.